Contents

Sending messages 2
Signs 4
Morse code 10
Braille code 12
Secret codes 14
Glossary 16

SENDING MESSAGES

We can send messages in lots of ways. We can talk on the telephone to send a message.

We can post a letter to send a message.

SIGNS

We don't have to talk or post a letter to send a message. We can send a message with signs.

What do these signs tell us?

5

Look all around. What signs can you see?

Signs tell us where we can go. They tell us where we can't go, too.

This boy can't hear or talk. He sends messages with his hands.

He makes this sign with his hand to say "yes".

MORSE CODE

You can send a message in code. This code is called Morse code.

Morse Code

A	•—		N	—•
B	—•••		O	———
C	—•—•		P	•——•
D	—••		Q	——•—
E	•		R	•—•
F	••—•		S	•••
G	——•		T	—
H	••••		U	••—
I	••		V	•••—
J	•———		W	•——
K	—•—		X	—••—
L	•—••		Y	—•——
M	——		Z	——••

Can you read this Morse code message?

—·—·   ———   —··   ·   ···

·—   ·—·   ·

··—·   ··—   —·

It says "Codes are fun."

11

BRAILLE CODE

This girl can't see but she can read.
She can read a code called Braille.

She can read Braille with her hands.

SECRET CODES

Secret messages are fun.

My Secret Code

A	B	C	D	E	F	G
1	2	3	4	5	6	7

H	I	J	K	L	M	N
8	9	10	11	12	13	14

O	P	Q	R	S	T	U
15	16	17	18	19	20	21

V	W	X	Y	Z
22	23	24	25	26

Can you read this secret message?
9 12-9-11-5 3-15-4-5-19!

It says "I like codes!".

Now make up a code to send a secret message.
Be a code-cracker!

Glossary

code
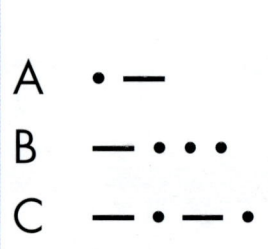

hands
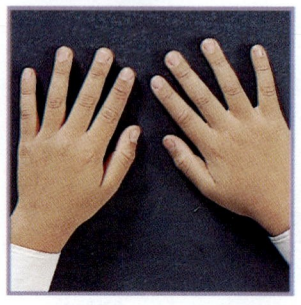

hear

message
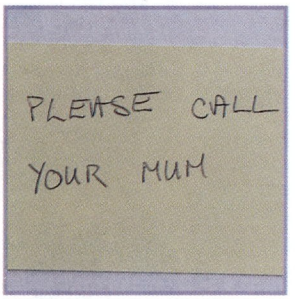

post

read

sign

talk

telephone